The Best Pet for Me

Is a RABBIT
a Good Pet for Me?

Melissa Raé Shofner

PowerKiDS press™

New York

Published in 2020 by The Rosen Publishing Group, Inc.
29 East 21st Street, New York, NY 10010

First Edition

Editor: Elizabeth Krajnik
Book Design: Rachel Rising

Photo Credits: Cover, pp. 1, 3, 6, 20 Eric Isselee/Shutterstock.com; Cover, pp. 1,3,4, 6, 8,10,12,14,16,18,20,22,23,24 (background) Anna_leni/Shutterstock.com; p. 4 Scorpp/Shutterstock.com; p. 5 Photobac/Shutterstock.com; p. 7 sirtravelalot/Shutterstock.com; p. 8 cynoclub/Shutterstock.com; p. 9 StockLite/Shutterstock.com; p. 10 marilyn barbone/Shutterstock.com; pp. 11, 12 Kuttelvaserova Stuchelova/Shutterstock.com; p. 13 Tyler Olson/Shutterstock.com; p. 14 ARTFULLY PHOTOGRAPHER/Shutterstock.com; p. 15 kai_foret/Shutterstock.com; p. 16 Jiri Vaclavek/Shutterstock.com; p. 17 Linas T/Shutterstock.com; p. 18 Africa Studio/Shutterstock.com; p. 19 Pentium5/Shutterstock.com; p. 21 Ijansempoi/Shutterstock.com; p. 22 JIANG HONGYAN/Shutterstock.com.

Library of Congress Cataloging-in-Publication Data

Names: Shofner, Melissa Raé, author.
Title: Is a rabbit a good pet for me? / Melissa Raé Shofner.
Description: New York, NY : PowerKids Press, [2020] | Series: The best pet for me | Includes index.
Identifiers: LCCN 2018055478| ISBN 9781725301160 (paperback) | ISBN 9781725301184 (library bound) | ISBN 9781725301177 (6 pack)
Subjects: LCSH: Rabbits–Juvenile literature. | Pets–Juvenile literature.
Classification: LCC SF453.2 .S54 2020 | DDC 632/.6932–dc23
LC record available at https://lccn.loc.gov/2018055478

Manufactured in the United States of America

CPSIA Compliance Information: Batch #CSPK19. For Further Information contact Rosen Publishing, New York, New York at 1-800-237-9932.

Contents

A Furry Friend

Many people have pets. Pets can be cute, cuddly, and fun to play with. A pet may even become another member of the family. Getting a pet can be **exciting**. However, there's a lot more to owning a pet than you might think.

What kind of pet do you think you'd like to have? If you'd like to get a rabbit, be ready to take on a big **responsibility**. You will need to feed, clean up after, and **groom** your rabbit. Do you think you're ready to get a pet rabbit? This book will help you decide if a rabbit is a good pet for you.

Before you get a pet rabbit, you should think about what you know about rabbits. Do you know what they eat? Do you know what kind of cage they need? Be prepared and do your **research**.

Choosing Your Rabbit

After you've decided to get a rabbit, you'll need to pick which breed, or kind, of rabbit you'd like to get. There are 49 recognized pet rabbit breeds. Rabbits come in many shapes, sizes, and colors.

The Netherland dwarf is one of the smallest rabbit breeds. It only weighs about 2.5 pounds (1.1 kg) when fully grown. One of the largest rabbit breeds, the Flemish giant, is usually about 14 pounds (6.4 kg) but can weigh up to 22 pounds (10 kg). You'll need to pick up your rabbit, so keep in mind how much it may weigh once it's an adult.

Flemish giant

Pet Report

Some rabbits don't mind being picked up and held, but many don't like to be handled. If your pet feels scared or uncomfortable, it might **scratch** or bite you.

If you decide to get a baby or young rabbit, make sure to spend time getting it used to being handled. Have an adult help you so that you don't scare or hurt your rabbit.

A Rabbit's Life

Having a rabbit is a lifetime **commitment**. Some rabbits can live up to 12 years. Are you prepared to take care of your rabbit for this long? If not, a rabbit might not be a good pet for you. It's unfair to your rabbit and your family members if you decide you don't want to take care of your pet anymore and they need to take on the responsibility.

It's also important to think about your daily activities before bringing home a new pet. Rabbits are most active in the early morning and early evening. Does this fit with your life?

Pet Report

You can buy your rabbit from a pet store or a **breeder**. However, many people prefer to adopt their rabbit from an animal shelter.

You may still need your parents' help taking care of your rabbit. That's OK, but don't make them do all the work.

Your Rabbit's Home

Before bringing your rabbit home, you'll need to think about where it'll live. Many people choose to keep their rabbit in a special type of cage called a hutch. Hutches are often quite large and can cost a lot of money.

You can also keep your rabbit in a regular cage. Keep in mind, however, that cages with wire bottoms can hurt your rabbit. You'll need to put a board in the bottom of your pet's cage so it has something solid to walk on. Make sure whatever home you choose for your rabbit has enough room for it to **stretch** and move around freely.

hutch

Pet Report

You should keep your rabbit away from other pets. Dogs and cats might scare or even attack your rabbit. This is something you should think about before getting a rabbit.

If you decide to keep your rabbit outside, make sure its hutch is out of the wind, rain, and direct sun. You should also have a plan to keep your rabbit indoors during colder weather.

Staying Healthy

Just like you go to the doctor for checkups, your rabbit will need to visit a veterinarian to stay healthy. A veterinarian is a special doctor just for pets. However, not all veterinarians know a lot about rabbits. You may need to find a special rabbit veterinarian.

Rabbits are social animals, which means they're happiest with other rabbits. Getting two rabbits is better than getting one, but you need to be sure you can care for both rabbits properly. You shouldn't keep two males together because they may fight. You also shouldn't keep males and females together unless they've been **spayed** or **neutered**.

Pet Report

Rabbits can have babies starting when they're very young. They can have up to 12 babies a month. You should have your rabbits spayed or neutered when they're about four months old.

Finding a rabbit veterinarian can take a long time. Visits to a rabbit vet may cost more than those to a regular veterinarian. Do your research before you get your rabbit so you're prepared.

Rabbit Food

Rabbits need a balanced **diet** of hay, fresh veggies and fruit, and rabbit **pellets**. Hay should make up 80 to 90 percent of your rabbit's diet. Timothy hay is one of the best hays for rabbits. You should feed your rabbit a mixture of three vegetables, such as bell peppers, brussels sprouts, and zucchini, each day. Rabbits should only eat fruit one or two times a week.

You should feed your adult rabbit about one-quarter cup of pellets each day. If your rabbit is smaller, give it fewer pellets. If your rabbit is young, you can feed it alfalfa pellets.

Pet Report

Your rabbit's teeth never stop growing. If they get too long, they can harm your rabbit. Giving your rabbit lots of hay and special wooden toys to chew on will help keep its teeth short and in good shape.

Your rabbit will need a food bowl, a water bottle, and a hayrack. Make sure your rabbit's water bottle is always full and that it has plenty of hay at all times.

15

Happy Hoppers

Rabbits need plenty of room to exercise. You should let your pet run around for a few hours each day in a safe place in your house. You can also buy a pen so your rabbit can stretch its legs outside. If your rabbit is in the house, move houseplants, wires, and other dangerous objects out of its reach so it doesn't chew them.

Rabbits love to chew. You should give your rabbit things to chew on, such as some types of branches, hay, cotton towels, and chew toys, to keep it from getting bored.

rabbit toy

Pet Report

You should brush your rabbit's fur regularly to keep it clean. You'll also need to **trim** your rabbit's nails. Ask a parent or your veterinarian for help so you don't hurt your bunny or get scratched.

If you let your rabbit play outside, make sure other animals can't get into its pen. Birds, dogs, and cats might attack your pet. Keep the pen covered and out of direct sunlight, and never leave your bunny outside alone.

Bunny Problems

Rabbits can be great pets, but they don't always stay out of trouble. Your rabbit needs a lot of attention, especially if you only have one rabbit. Rabbits and their owners form close bonds. However, if your rabbit isn't given enough attention and exercise, it can act out by chewing, biting, and scratching. Bunnies can also wreck things around your home if you don't watch them carefully.

Rabbits are clean animals, but they create a lot of waste. If you don't clean their cage or hutch regularly, it can become smelly. You should clean your rabbit's cage at least weekly.

litter box

Pet Report

Many rabbits can be trained to use a litter box. Keep a litter box in your bunny's cage or hutch. You should clean your rabbit's litter box at least once a day.

GARFIELD COUNTY
LIBRARIES

04/28/2023
Carbondale Branch Library
Need to renew?
970-963-2889
www.gcpld.org

TITLE   **Caring for rabbits / by**

BARCODE   **1220005837616**

DUE DATE   **05-19-23**

You just saved an estimated $25.99
by using the Library today.

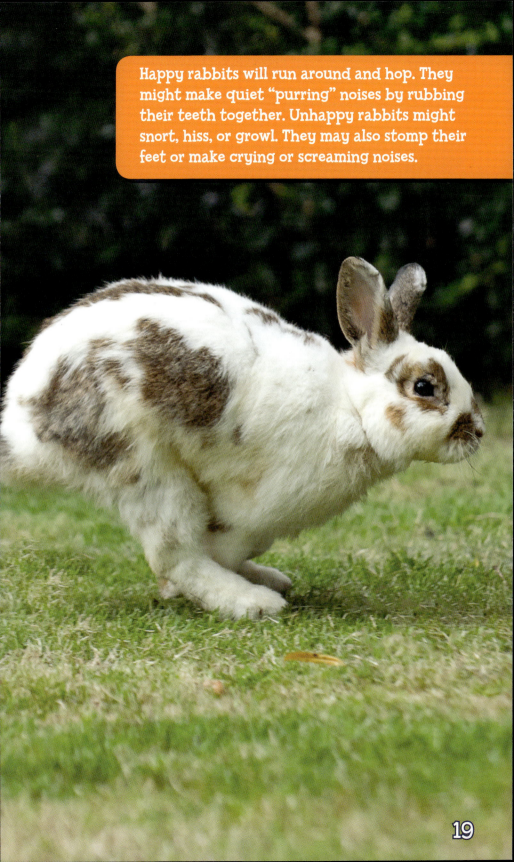

Happy rabbits will run around and hop. They might make quiet "purring" noises by rubbing their teeth together. Unhappy rabbits might snort, hiss, or growl. They may also stomp their feet or make crying or screaming noises.

You and Your Rabbit

Owning a pet rabbit can be a lot of fun. Your bunny may be another member of the family. It can be exciting to watch your rabbit run around and hop. However, it's important to remember that becoming a pet owner is a big responsibility. Your rabbit will depend on you for everything: food, water, shelter, and exercise.

You'll need to groom your rabbit and clean its cage regularly. Your rabbit needs plenty of time to exercise and explore so it doesn't get bored. Do you think you have what it takes to keep a rabbit happy and healthy? If so, a rabbit might be a good pet for you.

Your pet rabbit can teach you a lot about being responsible.

What You'll Need

Cost: $5 to $100 depending on breed and place of purchase

Cage or hutch: $30 to $650

Playpen: $40 to $60

Bedding: $4 to $25 depending on brand and quantity

Litter box: $5 to $10

Litter: $6 to $20 depending on brand and quantity

Food dish: $3 to $12

Water bottle: $5 to $20

Hayrack: $5 to $13

Vegetables and fruits: $20

Timothy hay: $5 to $20 depending on brand and quantity

Pellets: $6 to $40 depending on brand and quantity

Chew toys: $2 to $12

Grooming kit: $4 to $8

Total estimated cost for beginning supplies:
$140 to $1,010

Glossary

breeder: A person who keeps animals to sell their young.

commitment: An agreement to do something.

diet: The food and drink an animal usually takes in.

exciting: Making someone feel energetic and eager to do something.

groom: To clean and care for an animal.

neuter: To remove the sex organs from a male animal.

pellet: A usually small, rounded piece of food.

research: The activity of getting information, or knowledge, about a subject.

responsibility: The quality or state of being in charge of someone or something.

scratch: To make a shallow and narrow cut in the skin with something sharp, such as fingernails or claws.

spay: To remove the sex organs from a female animal.

stretch: To reach out or extend the body or limbs.

trim: To remove something by cutting.

Index

A
adult, 6, 7
alfalfa pellets, 14
animal shelter, 8

B
babies, 7, 12
bedding, 22
birds, 17
breed, 6, 22
breeder, 8

C
cage, 5, 10, 18, 20, 22
cats, 10, 17

D
diet, 14
doctor, 12
dogs, 10, 17

E
evening, 8
exercise, 18, 20

F
family, 4, 8, 20
feet, 19
females, 12
Flemish giant, 6
food, 14, 15, 20, 22
fruit, 14, 22
fur, 16

H
hay, 14, 15, 16, 22
hutch, 10, 11, 18, 22

L
litter box, 18, 22

M
males, 12
morning, 8

N
nails, 16
Netherland dwarf, 6
noises, 19

P
pellets, 14, 22
pen, 16, 17, 22
pet store, 8

R
research, 5, 13
responsibility, 4, 8, 20

T
teeth, 14, 19
timothy hay, 14, 22
toys, 14, 16, 22

V
vegetables, 14, 22
veterinarian, 12, 13, 16

W
waste, 18
water, 15, 20, 22
weather, 11
wire, 10, 16

Websites

Due to the changing nature of Internet links, PowerKids Press has developed an online list of websites related to the subject of this book. This site is updated regularly. Please use this link to access the list:
www.powerkidslinks.com/bpfm/rabbit